How Sound Moves

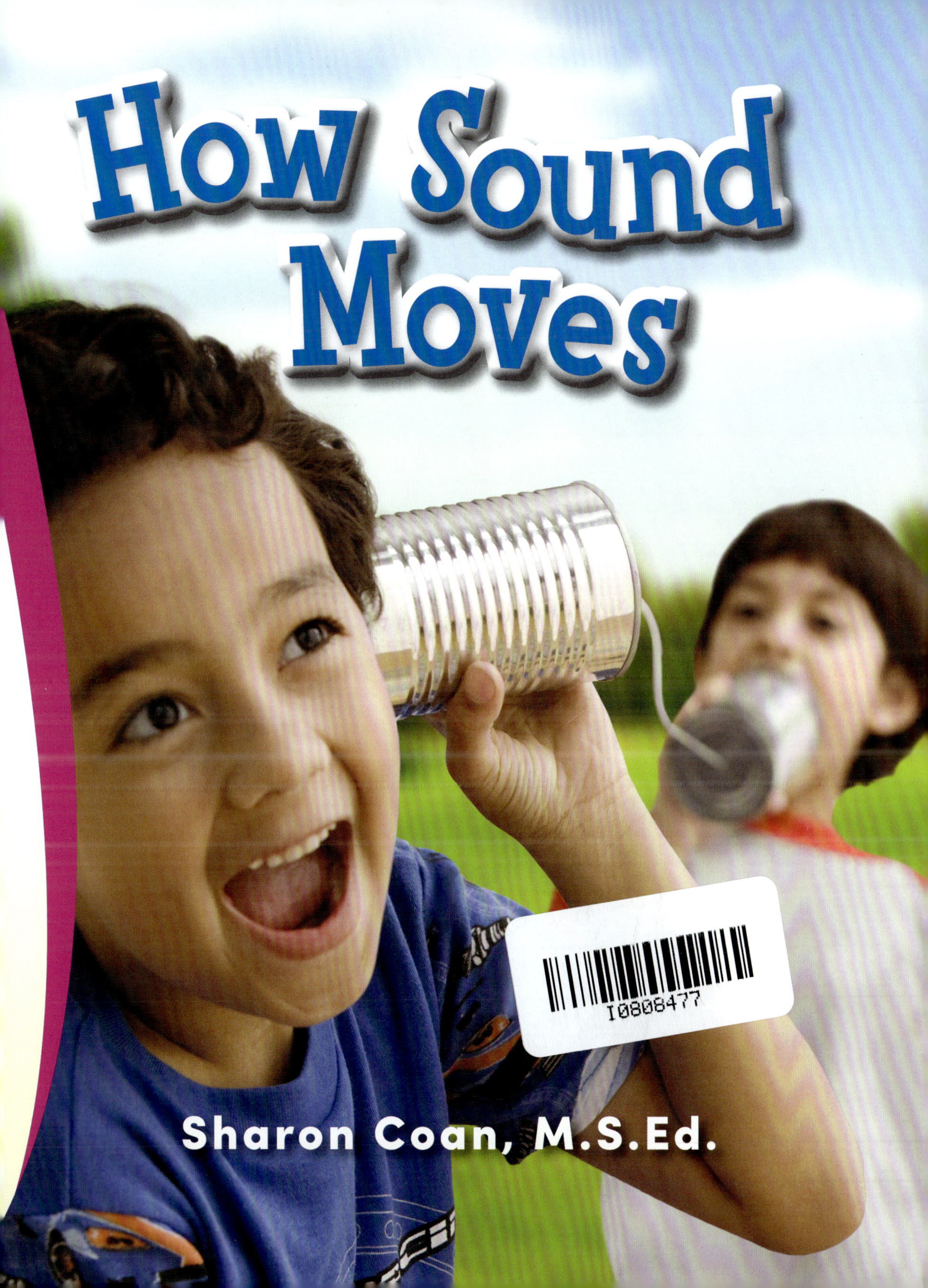

Sharon Coan, M.S.Ed.

Consultants

Sally Creel, Ed.D.
Curriculum Consultant

Leann Iacuone, M.A.T., NBCT, ATC
Riverside Unified School District

Jill Tobin
California Teacher of the Year
Semi-Finalist
Burbank Unified School District

Image Credits: Cover & p.1 KidStock/agefotostock; p.11 BSIP SA/Alamy; p.7 Katherine Frey/The Washington Post/Blend Images/Alamy; p.12 KidStock/agefotostock; pp.20–21 (illustrations) Janelle Bell-Martin; all other images from Shutterstock.

Library of Congress Cataloging-in-Publication Data

Coan, Sharon, author.
How sound moves / Sharon Coan, M.S.Ed.; consultants, Sally Creel, Ed.D. curriculum consultant, Leann Iacuone, M.A.T., NBCT, ATC Riverside Unified School District, Jill Tobin, California Teacher of the Year semi-finalist Burbank Unified School District.
pages cm.
Summary: "Sounds are all around us. Some sounds are loud. Others are quiet. Some sounds are high. Others are low. The sounds that we hear travel as sound waves." — Provided by publisher.
Audience: K to grade 3.
Includes index.
ISBN 978-1-4807-4564-3 (pbk.)
ISBN 978-1-4807-5054-8 (ebook)
1. Sound—Juvenile literature.
2. Sound-waves—uvenile literature. I. Title.
QC243.C63 2015
534—dc23
2014013149

Teacher Created Materials
5301 Oceanus Drive
Huntington Beach, CA 92649-1030
http://www.tcmpub.com

ISBN 978-1-4807-4564-3

Printed by: VIN#973
Printed In: China
PO11140

Table of Contents

Boom! Boom! Boom!

You hear the booming noise of a deep drum.

How does the sound reach you, and how do you know what it is?

Sound Waves

A drummer hits a drumstick against a **drumhead** to make it **vibrate** (VAHY-breyt).

To vibrate is to move back and forth quickly.

When the person hits the drumhead, it vibrates and makes sound.

The **vibrations** (vahy-BREY-shuhns) bump the air and start a **sound wave**.

The sound wave travels through the air to your ear.

This drum makes sound waves.

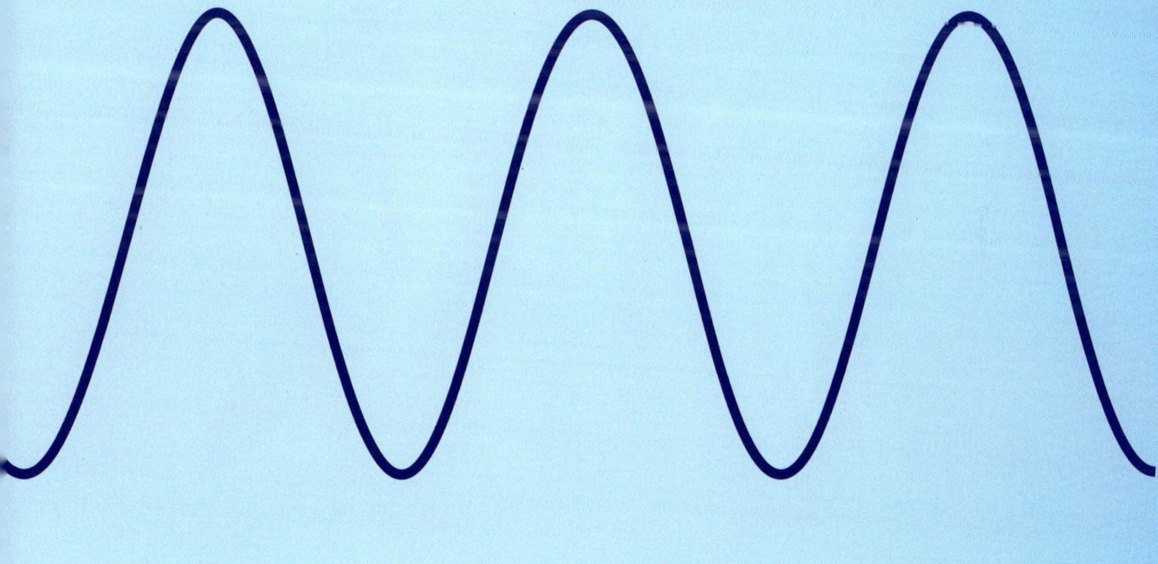

Hearing Sound

The wave quickly reaches your ear and goes inside the **canal**.

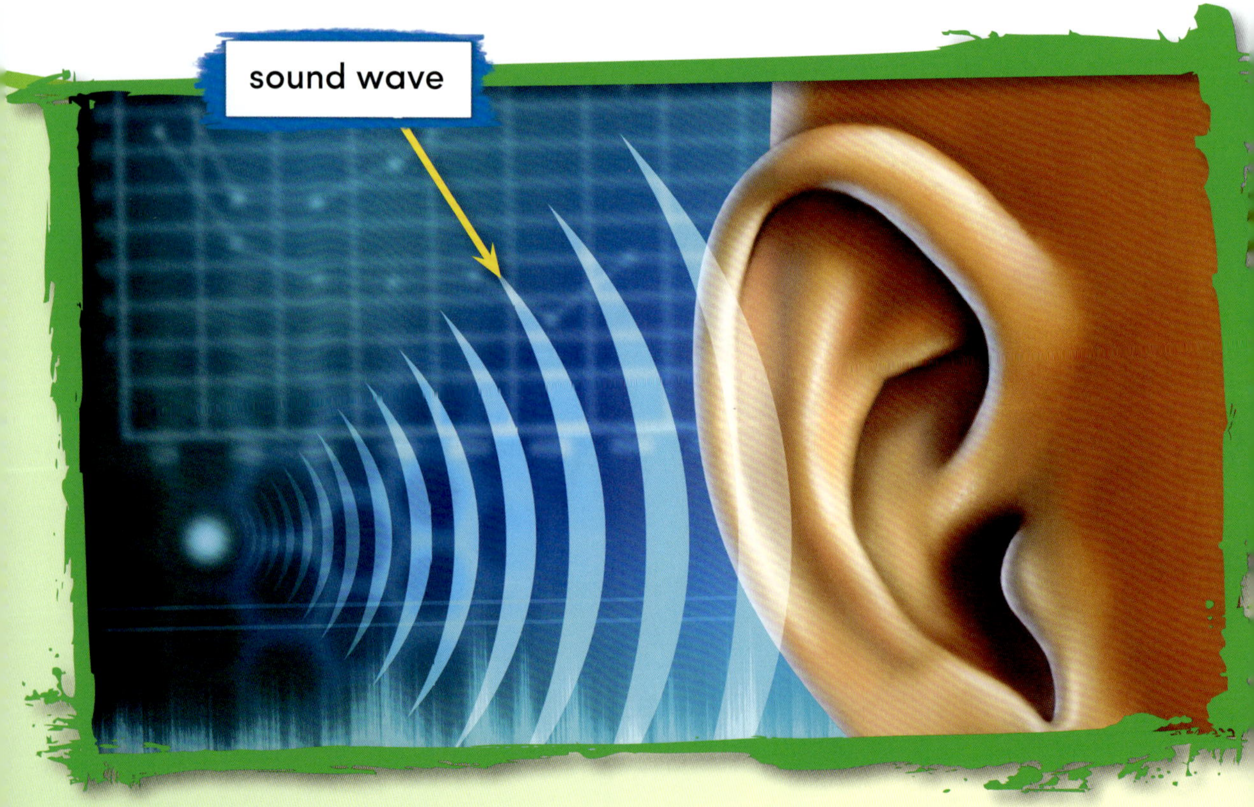

It bumps a little drum there called an **eardrum**.

Inside Your Ear

Your eardrum is a small flap of skin in your ear. Sound waves make it vibrate.

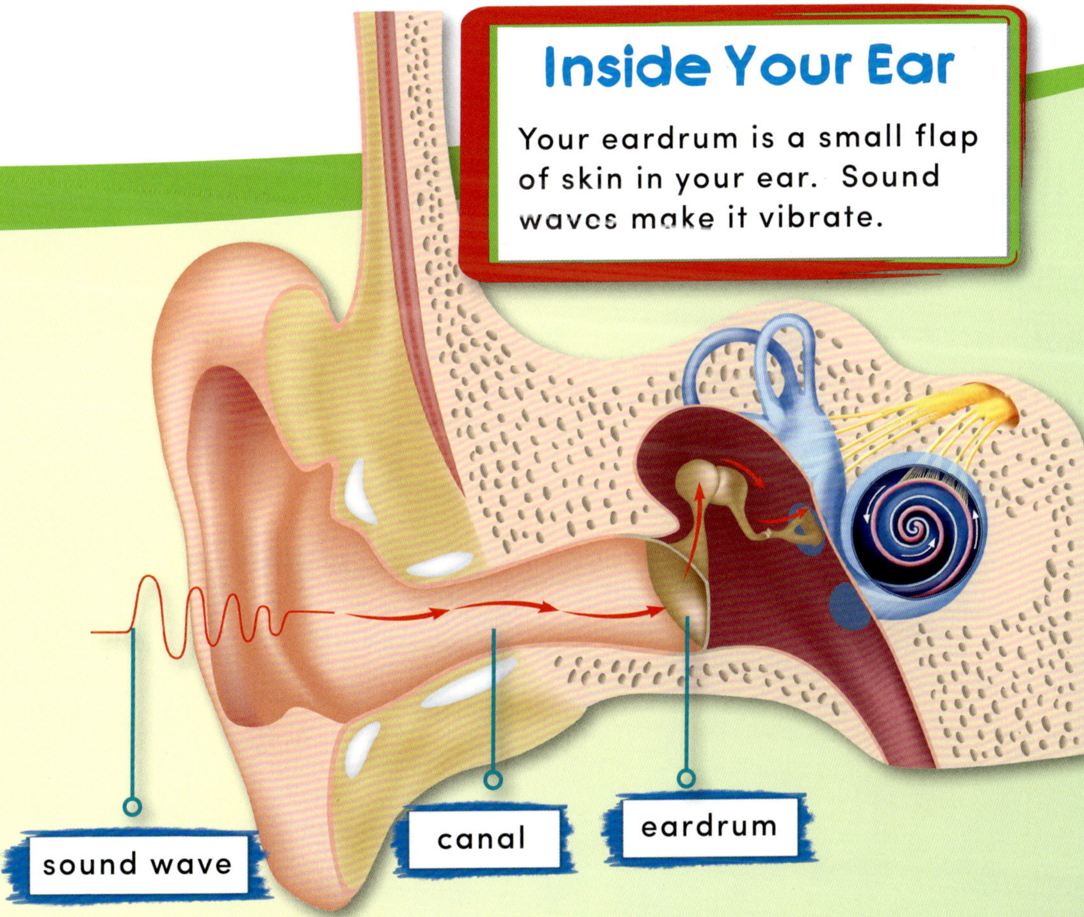

The eardrum sends a message to your brain.

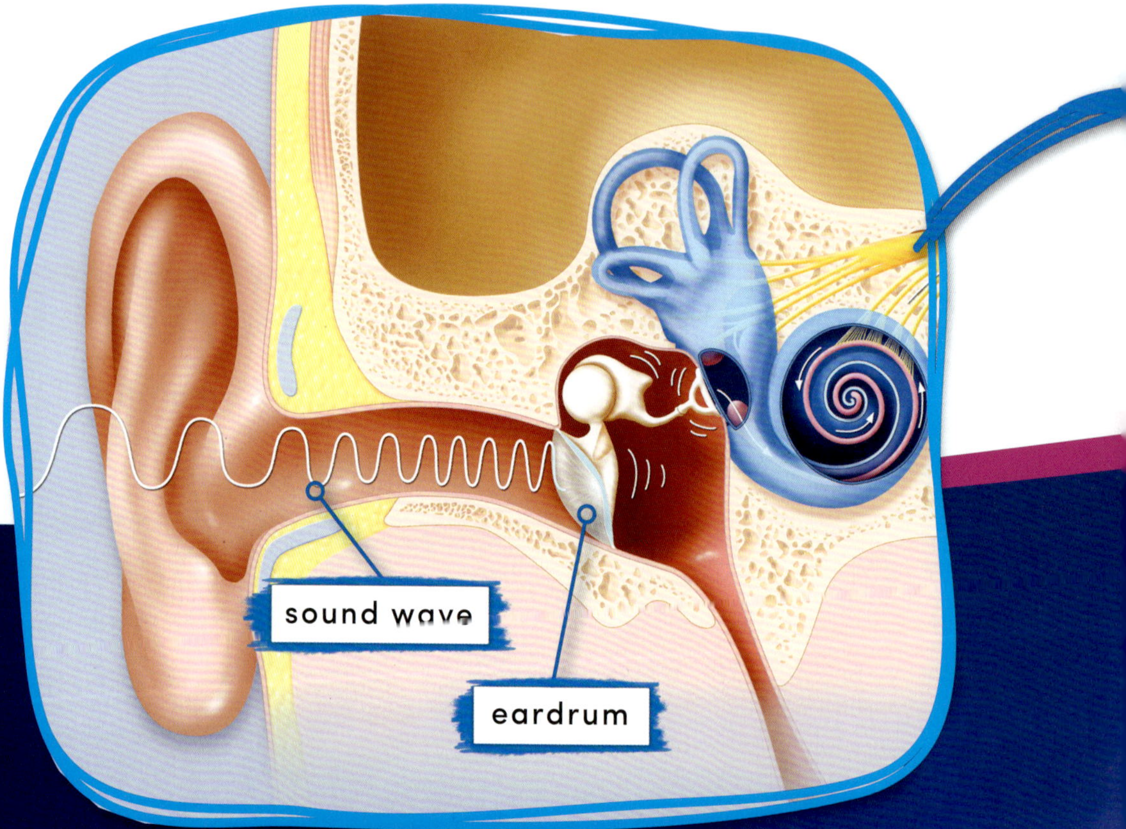

Your brain hears the boom and tells you that the boom is the sound of a drum.

Volume: How Loud Is It?

Some sounds are loud and move in tall waves, such as a drum's boom.

Volume

Volume (VOL-yoom) tells how loud a sound is. The higher the volume, the louder the sound.

Quiet sounds have short waves.

Some sounds are quiet and move in short waves.

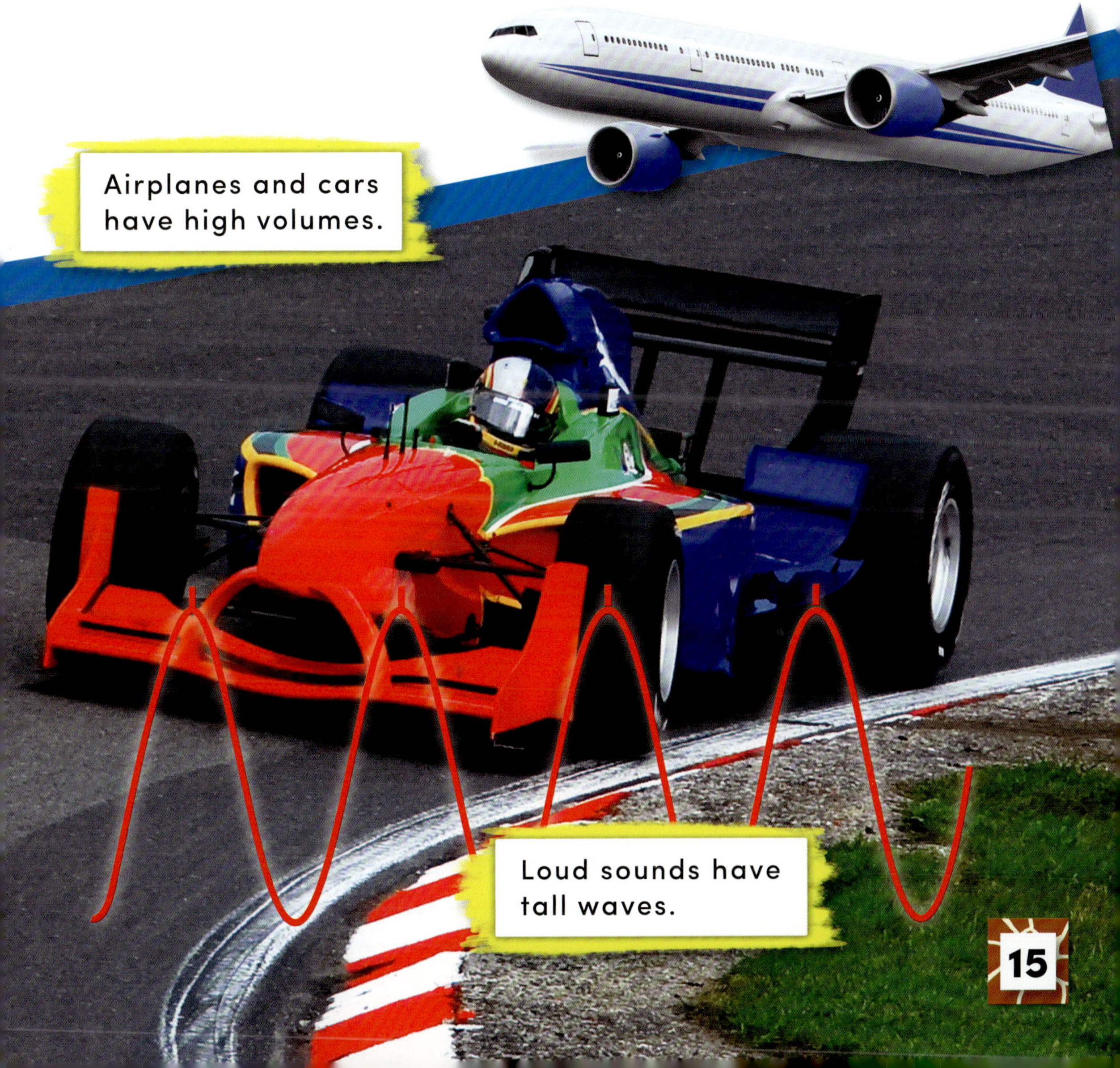

Airplanes and cars have high volumes.

Loud sounds have tall waves.

Pitch: How High Is It?

Some sounds are high and move in waves that are close together.

Tea kettles make high sounds.

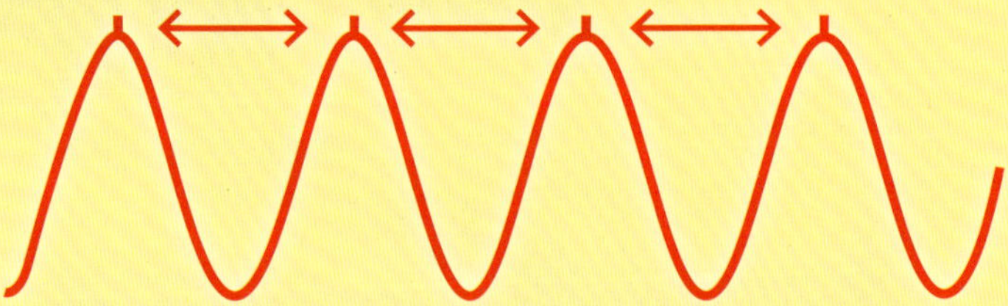

Waves are closer together when the pitch is high.

Some sounds are low and move in waves that are far apart. A deep drum boom is like this, too.

Pitch

The **pitch** tells how high or low a sound is.

Lions make low sounds.

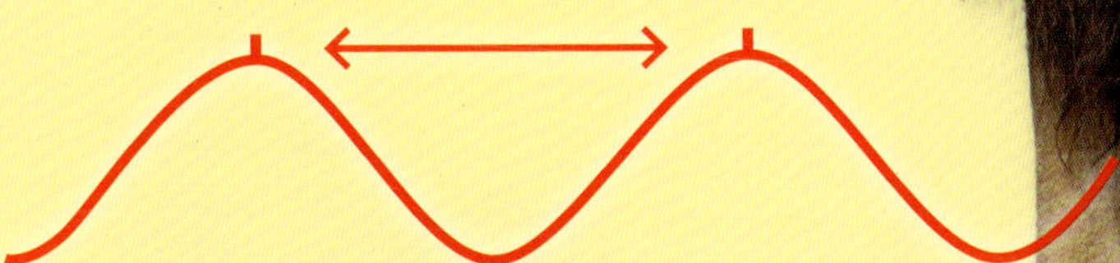

Waves are far apart when the pitch is low.

Sounds Are Everywhere

Close your eyes and listen closely to the noises around you. You can tell that sound waves are everywhere.

Dogs can make sounds with high and low pitches.

What is their volume?
What is their pitch?

Birds can make many sounds.

Fire engines can make loud sounds.

Let's Do Science!

How is sound made? Try this and see!

What to Get

- a round container, such as a cookie tin, a bucket, or a large can
- masking tape
- pencil
- scissors
- tissues

What to Do

1. Tightly stretch strips of tape across the top of the container. Cover it with two layers of tape.

2. Wrap tissue around the end of a pencil. Tape it in place.

3. Gently hit the tape with the pencil. What do you hear? What do you see?

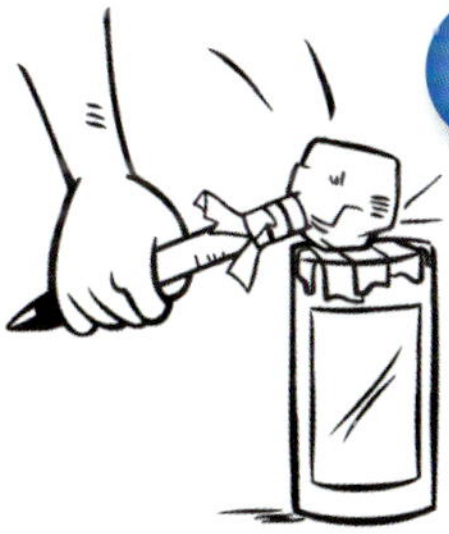

4. Place your hand on the container after you hit it. What do you feel?

Glossary

canal—the tube that leads into the ear

drumhead—part of the drum that is hit

eardrum—thin piece of skin in the ear that vibrates when sound waves reach it

pitch—how high or low a sound is

sound wave—wave that cannot be seen that is formed when sound is made

vibrate—move back and forth very fast

vibrations—fast back and forth movements

volume—how loud or soft a sound is

Index

Your Turn!

So Many Sounds

Listen for the sounds around you. Make a chart. Label the columns *Loud*, *Quiet*, *High*, and *Low*. List the sounds you hear in the correct column.